GRAPHIC LIBRARY ®

GRAPHIC SCIENCE

THE ATTRACTIVE STORY OF MAGNETISM

WITH MAX AXIOM SUPER SCIENTIST

by Andrea Gianopoulos

illustrated by Cynthia Martin and Barbara Schulz

Consultant:
Leslie Flynn, PhD
Science Education
University of Minnesota

Capstone press ®

Mankato, Minnesota

Graphic Library is published by Capstone Press,
151 Good Counsel Drive, P.O. Box 669, Mankato, Minnesota 56002.
www.capstonepress.com

Printed in the United States of America

1 2 3 4 5 6 12 11 10 09 08 07

Library of Congress Cataloging-in-Publication Data
Gianopoulos, Andrea.
The attractive story of magnetism with Max Axiom, super scientist / by Andrea Gianopoulos; illustrated by Cynthia Martin and Barbara Schulz.
p. cm.—(Graphic library. Graphic science)
Summary: "In graphic novel format, follows the adventures of Max Axiom as he explains the science behind magnetism"—Provided by publisher.
Includes bibliographical references and index.
ISBN-13: 978-1-4296-0141-2 (hardcover)
ISBN-10: 1-4296-0141-8 (hardcover)
1. Magnetism—Juvenile literature. 2. Magnets—Juvenile literature. 3. Adventure stories—Juvenile literature. I. Martin, Cynthia, 1961- ill. II. Schulz, Barbara, ill. III. Title. IV. Series.
QC753.7.G53 2008
538—dc22 2007002262

Art Director and Designer
Bob Lentz

Cover Artist
Tod Smith

Colorist
Krista Ward

Editor
Christopher L. Harbo

TABLE OF CONTENTS

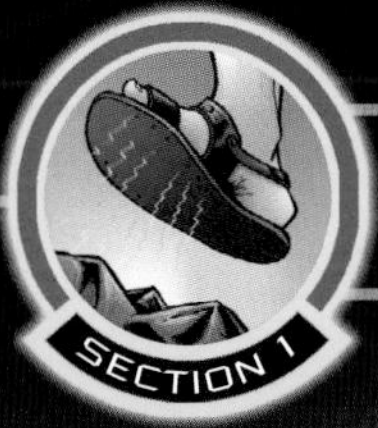
SECTION 1

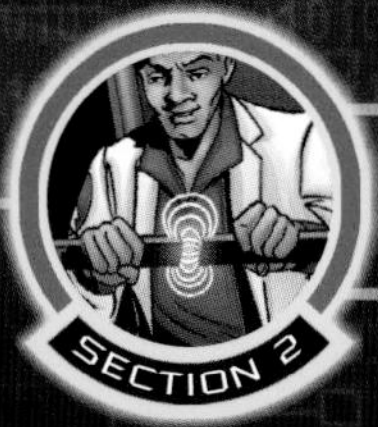
SECTION 2

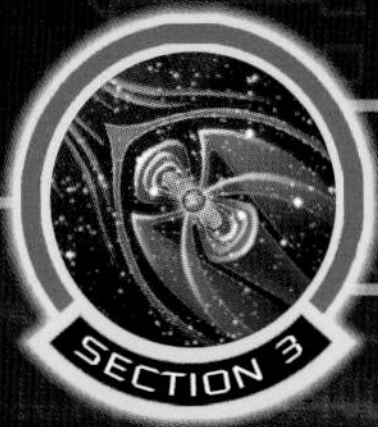
SECTION 3

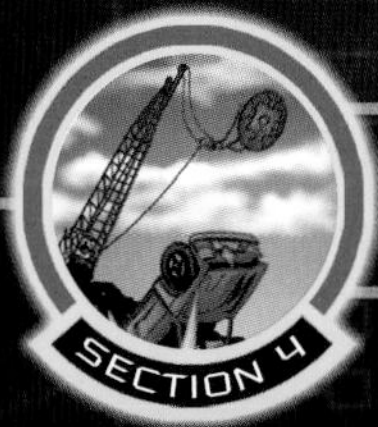
SECTION 4

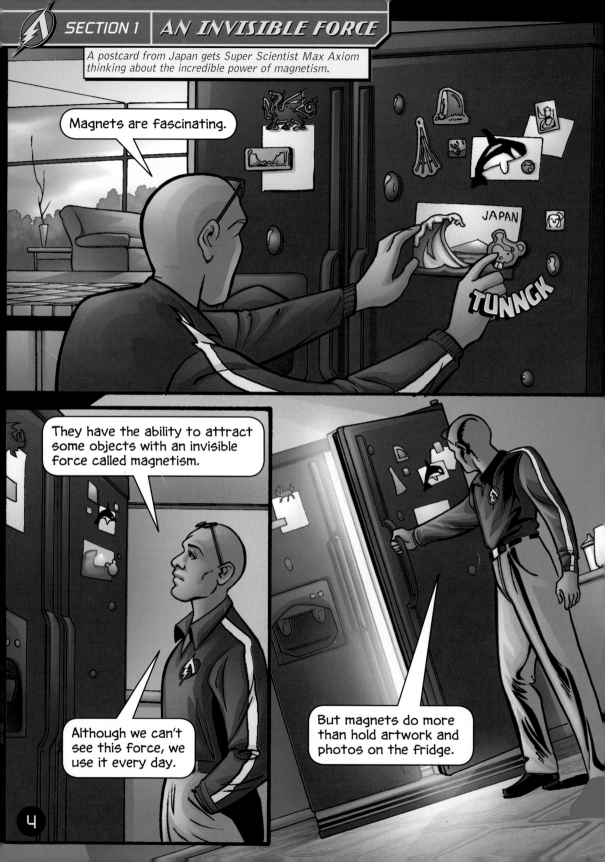

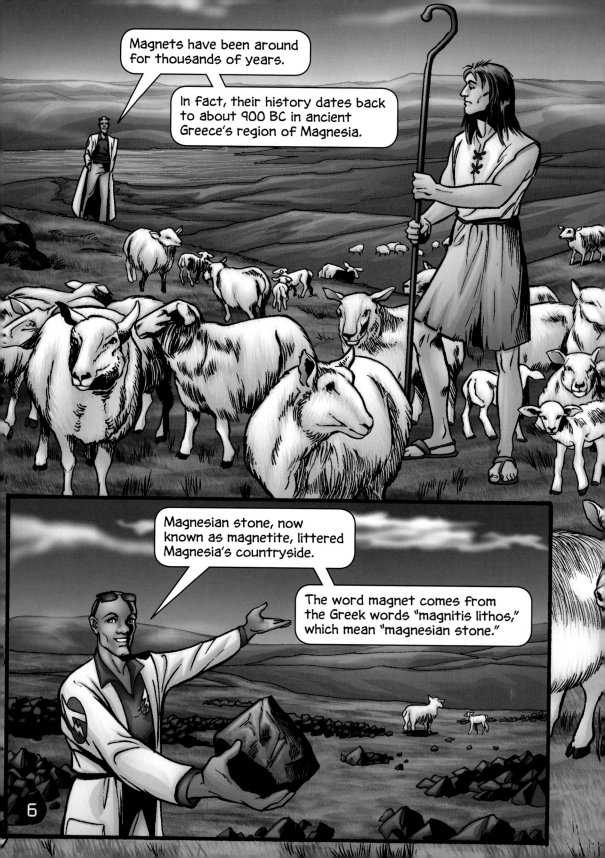

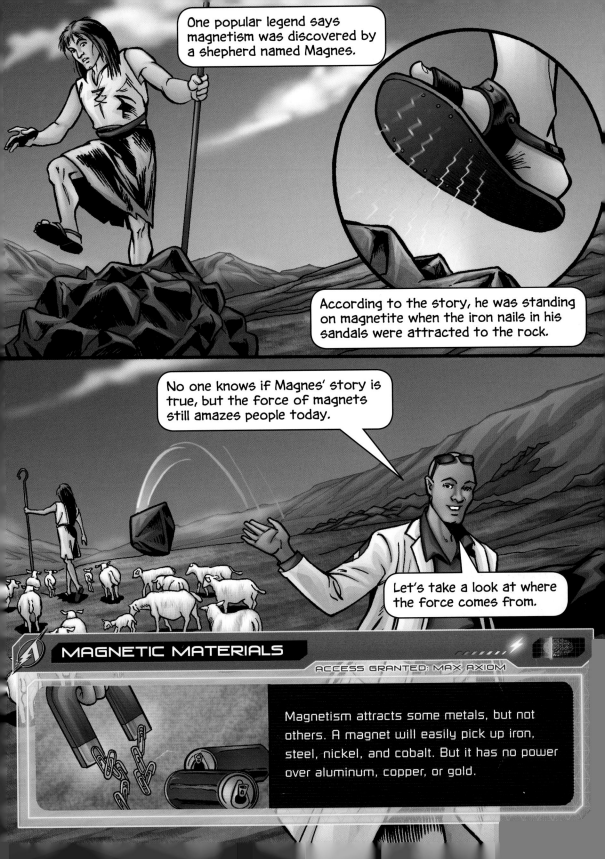

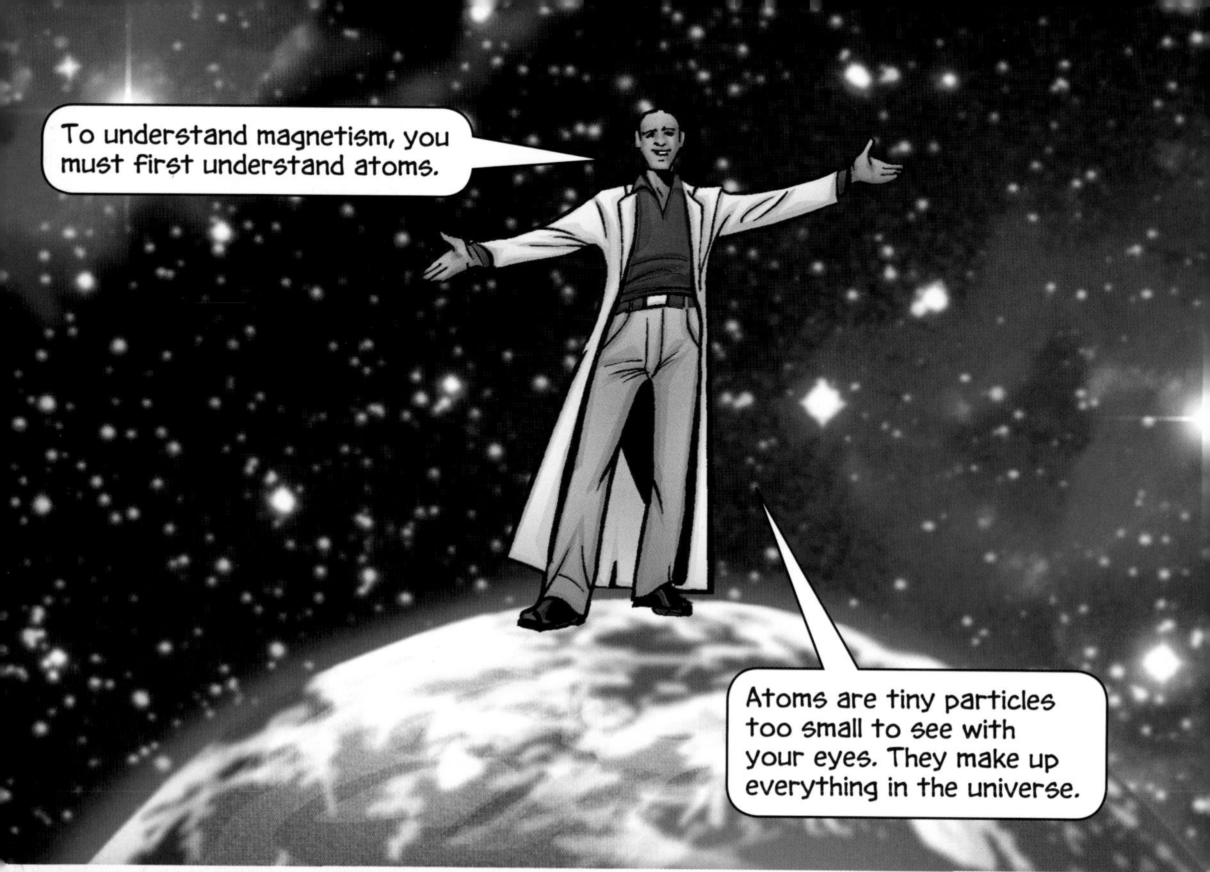
To understand magnetism, you must first understand atoms.
Atoms are tiny particles too small to see with your eyes. They make up everything in the universe.

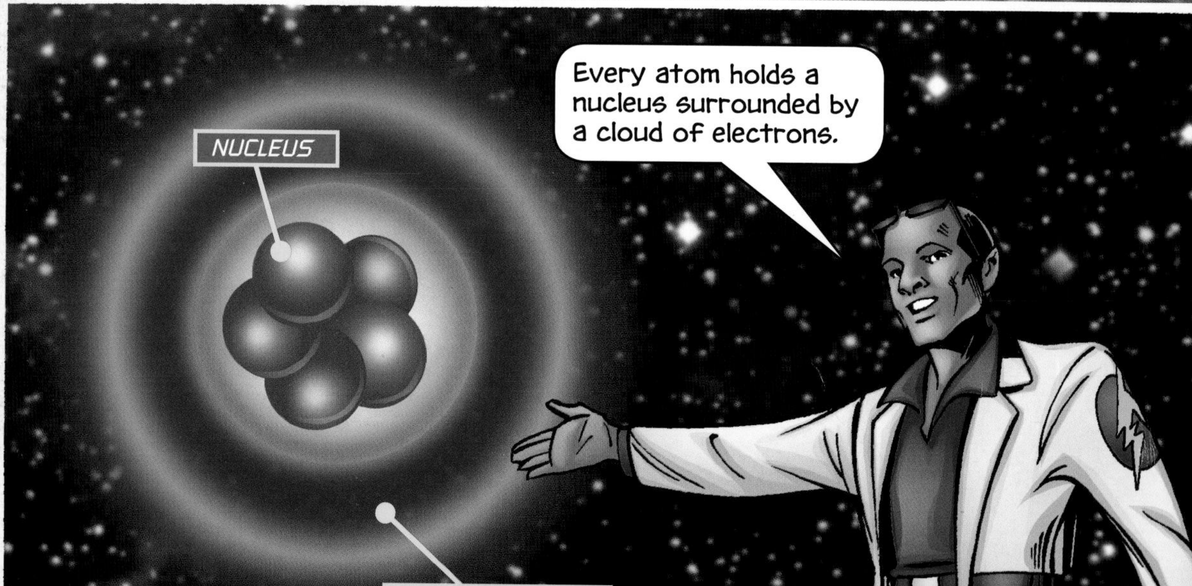
Every atom holds a nucleus surrounded by a cloud of electrons.
NUCLEUS
ELECTRON CLOUD

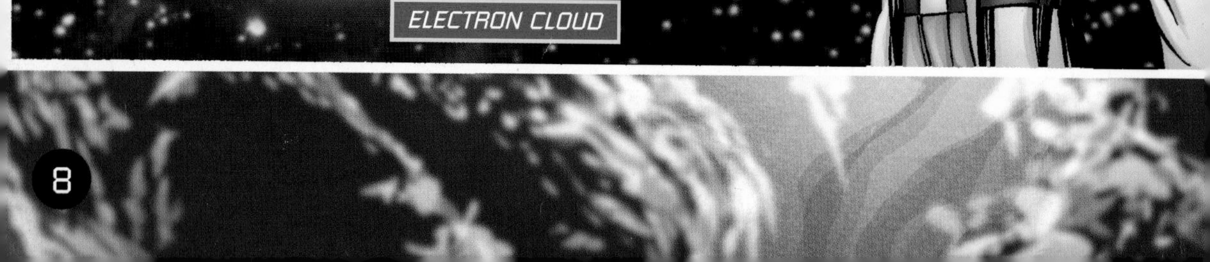

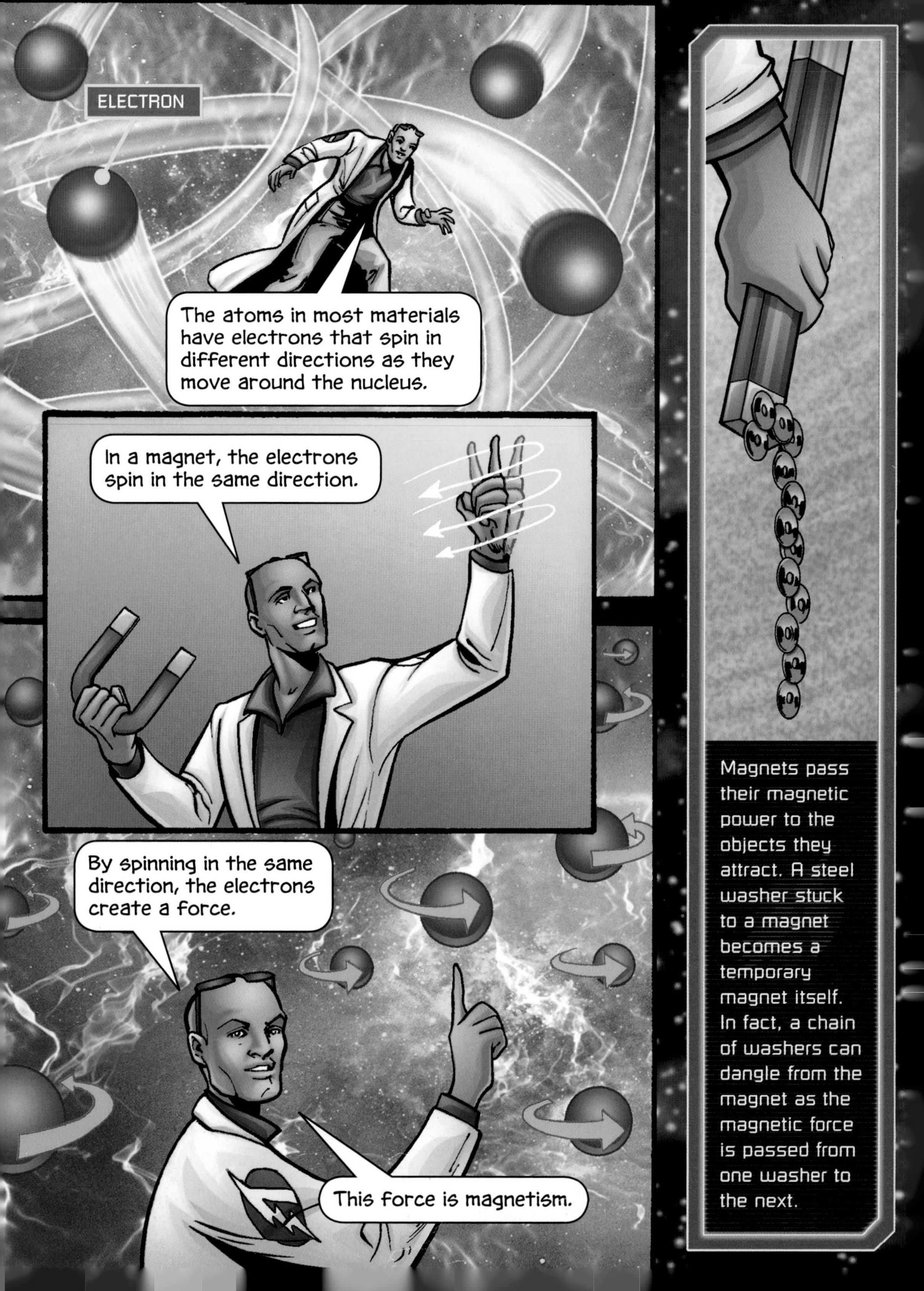
ELECTRON
The atoms in most materials have electrons that spin in different directions as they move around the nucleus.
In a magnet, the electrons spin in the same direction.
By spinning in the same direction, the electrons create a force.
This force is magnetism.
Magnets pass their magnetic power to the objects they attract. A steel washer stuck to a magnet becomes a temporary magnet itself. In fact, a chain of washers can dangle from the magnet as the magnetic force is passed from one washer to the next.

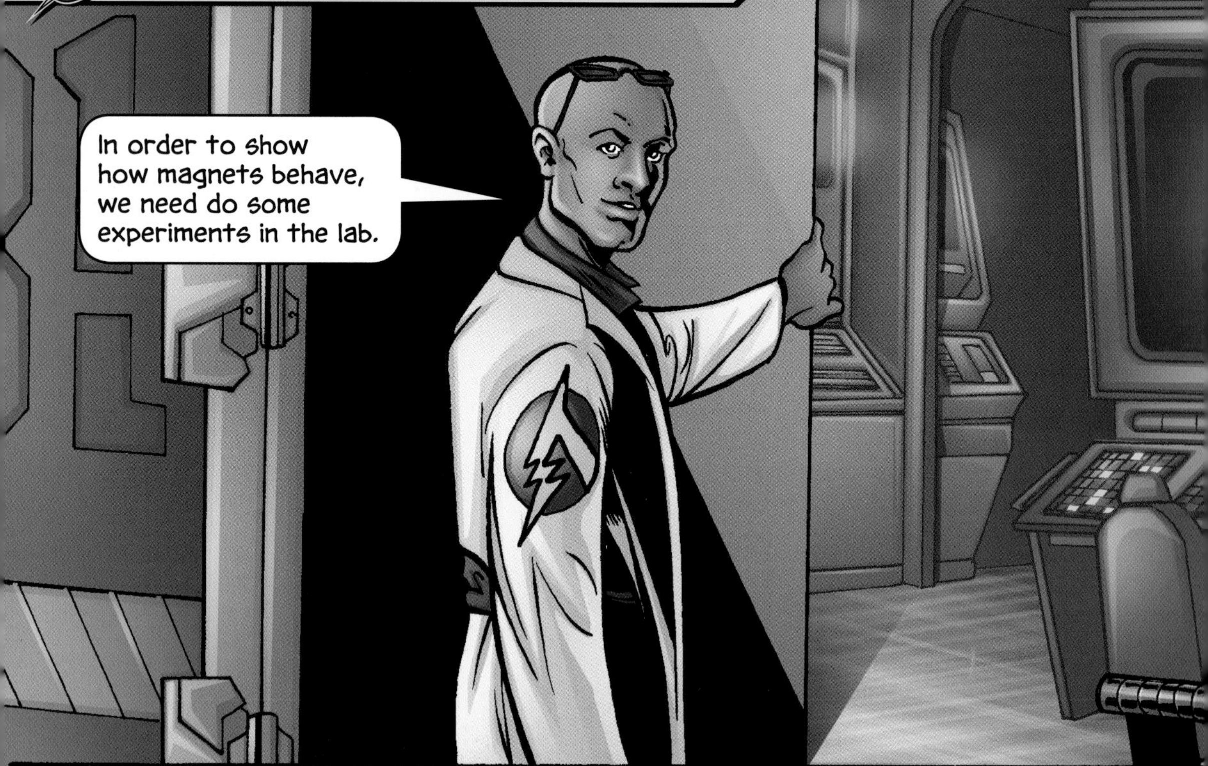
In order to show how magnets behave, we need do some experiments in the lab.

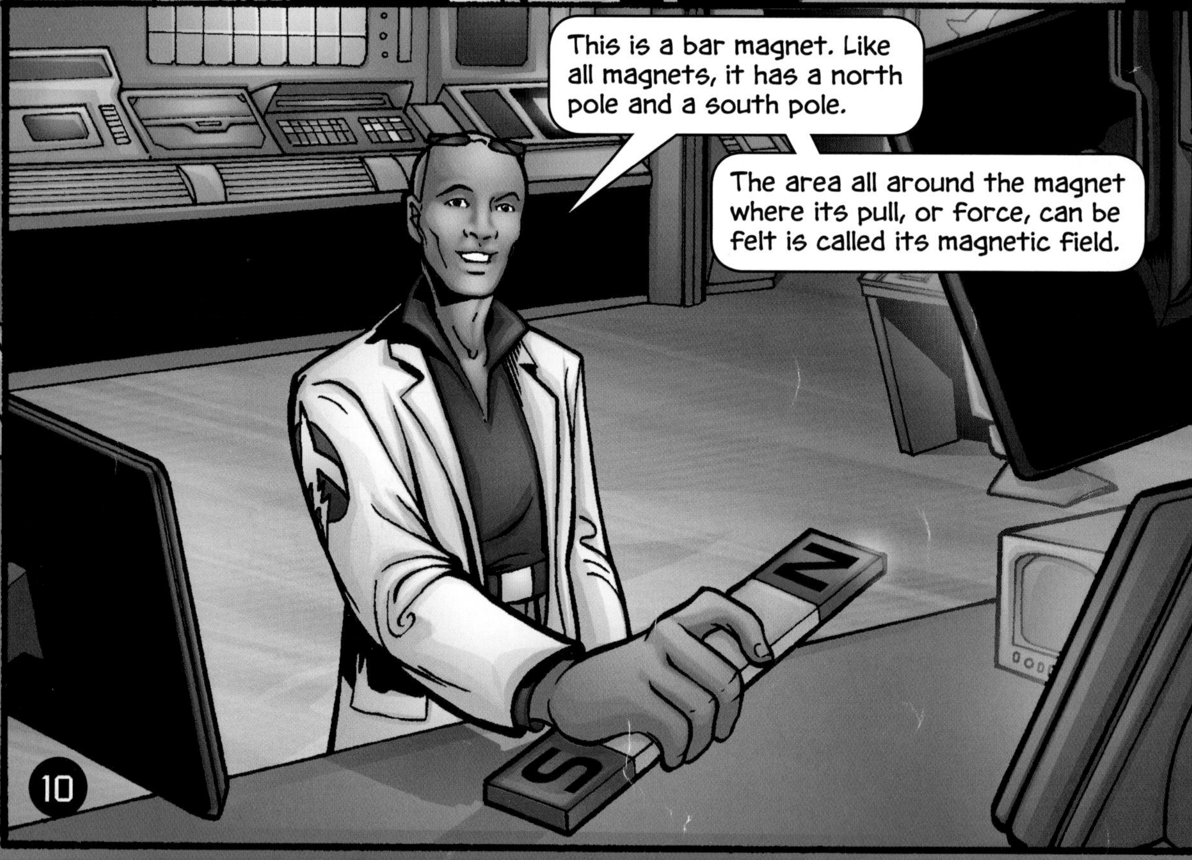
This is a bar magnet. Like all magnets, it has a north pole and a south pole.
The area all around the magnet where its pull, or force, can be felt is called its magnetic field.
N
S

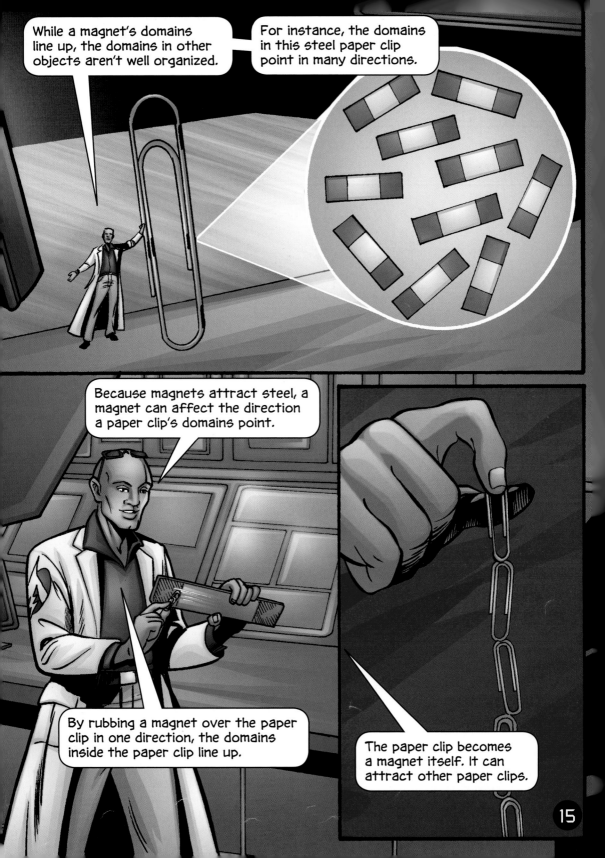

MAGNETS IN SPACE

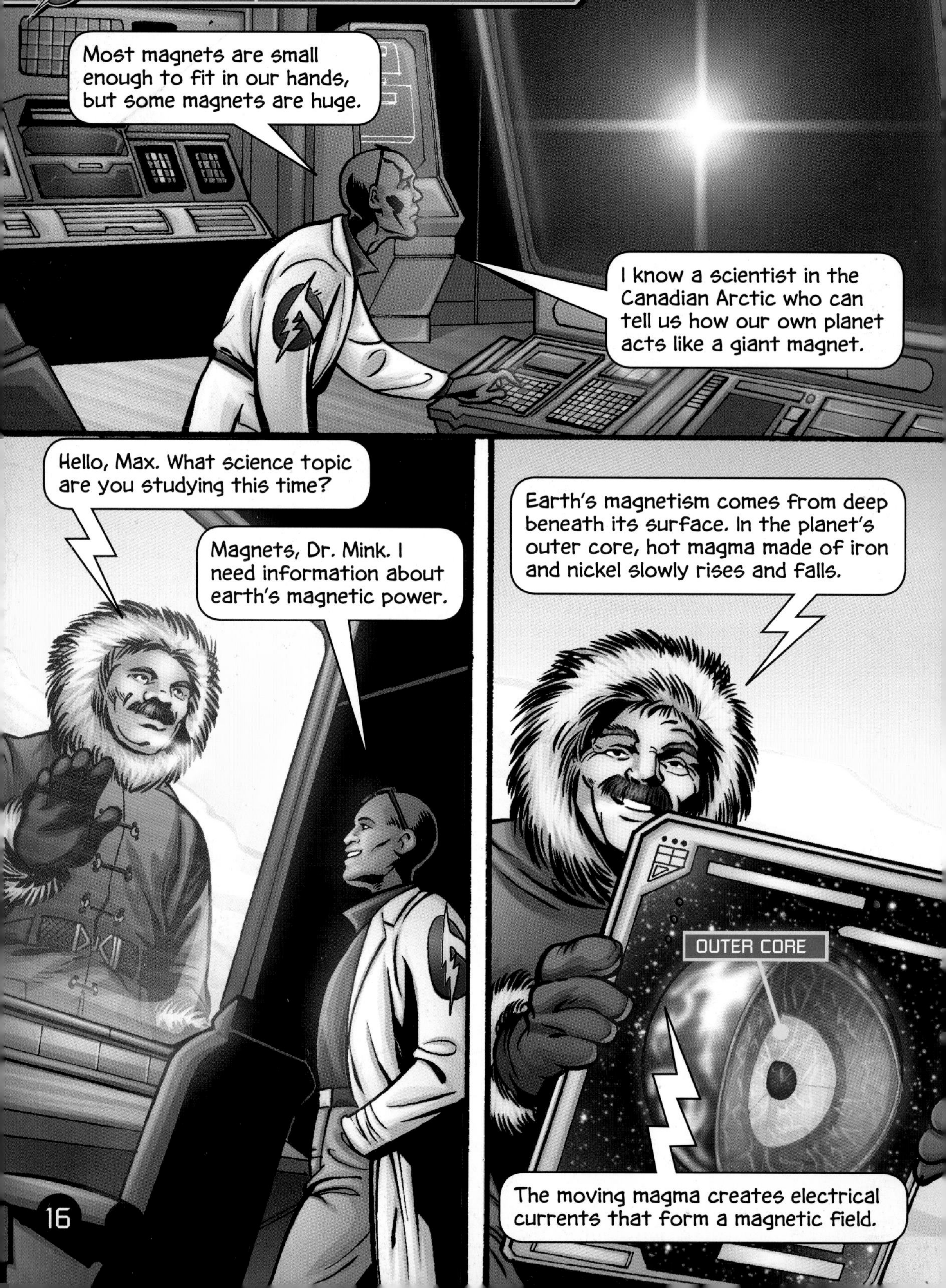
Most magnets are small enough to fit in our hands, but some magnets are huge.
I know a scientist in the Canadian Arctic who can tell us how our own planet acts like a giant magnet.
Hello, Max. What science topic are you studying this time?
Magnets, Dr. Mink. I need information about earth's magnetic power.
Earth's magnetism comes from deep beneath its surface. In the planet's outer core, hot magma made of iron and nickel slowly rises and falls.
OUTER CORE
The moving magma creates electrical currents that form a magnetic field.

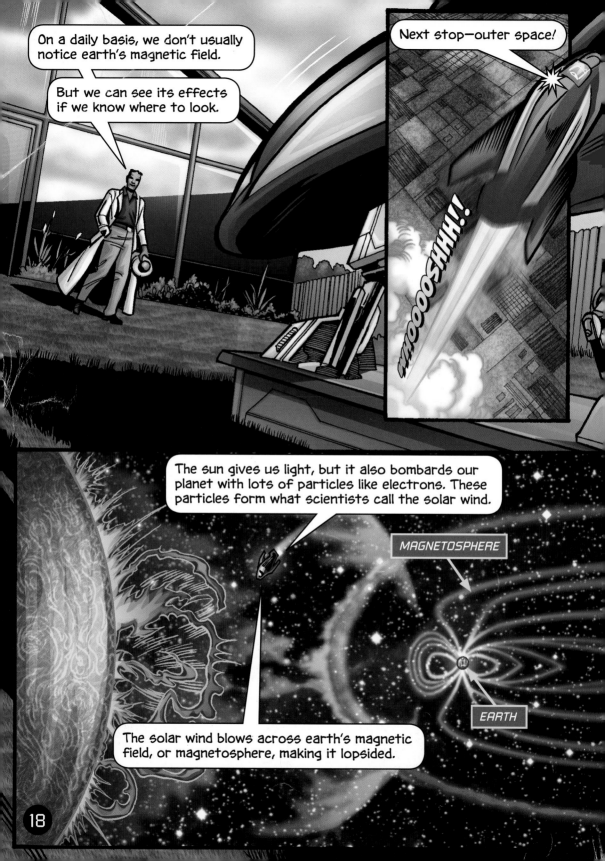

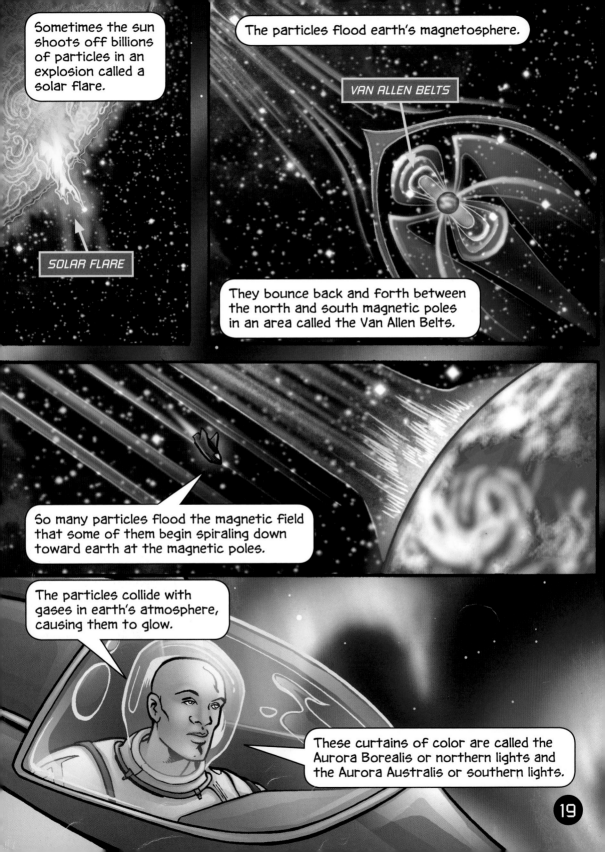

Sometimes the sun shoots off billions of particles in an explosion called a solar flare.

SOLAR FLARE

The particles flood earth's magnetosphere.

VAN ALLEN BELTS

They bounce back and forth between the north and south magnetic poles in an area called the Van Allen Belts.

So many particles flood the magnetic field that some of them begin spiraling down toward earth at the magnetic poles.

The particles collide with gases in earth's atmosphere, causing them to glow.

These curtains of color are called the Aurora Borealis or northern lights and the Aurora Australis or southern lights.

FINDING EAST

Finding north and south on a compass is easy. But what about east or west? Finding these directions is easier than you think. To find east, hold the compass level and rotate it so the letter E is on top. Now, slowly turn your body until the red tip of the needle points to the letter N. When it does, you are facing east.

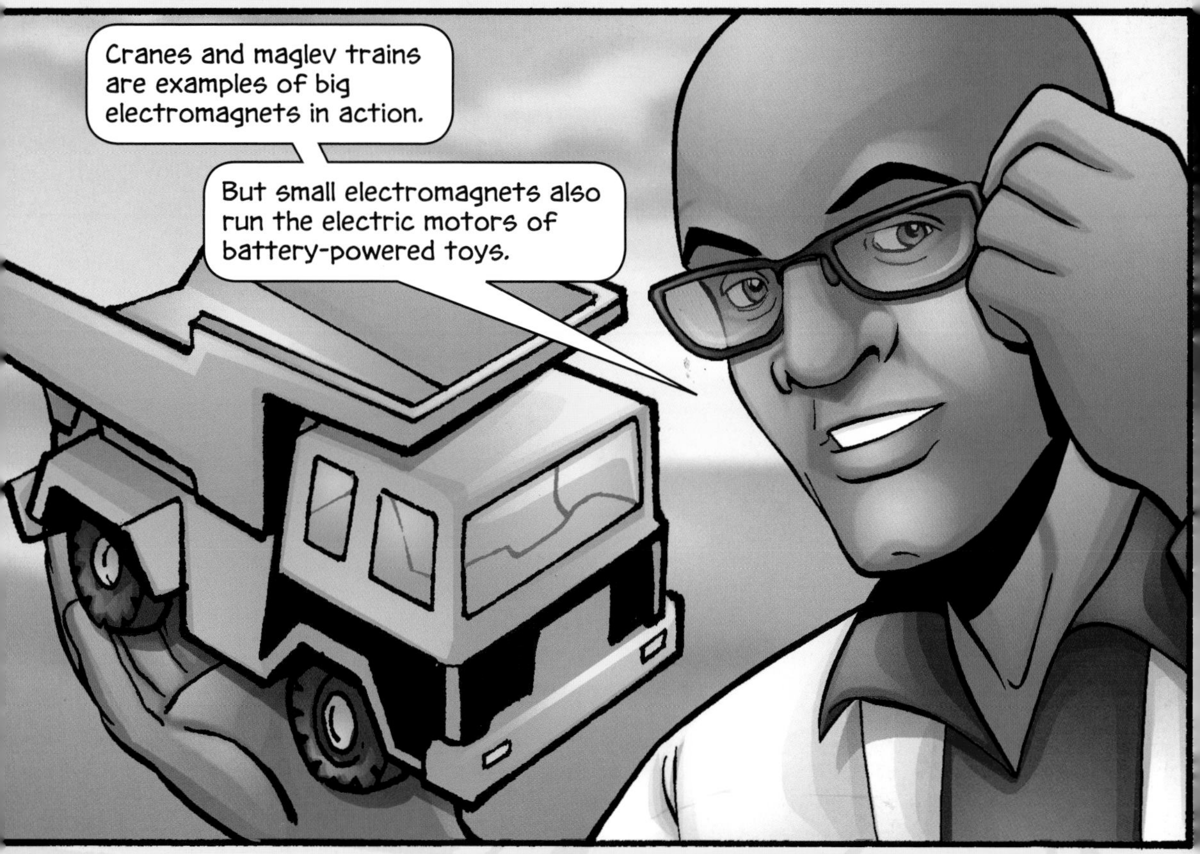
Cranes and maglev trains are examples of big electromagnets in action.
But small electromagnets also run the electric motors of battery-powered toys.

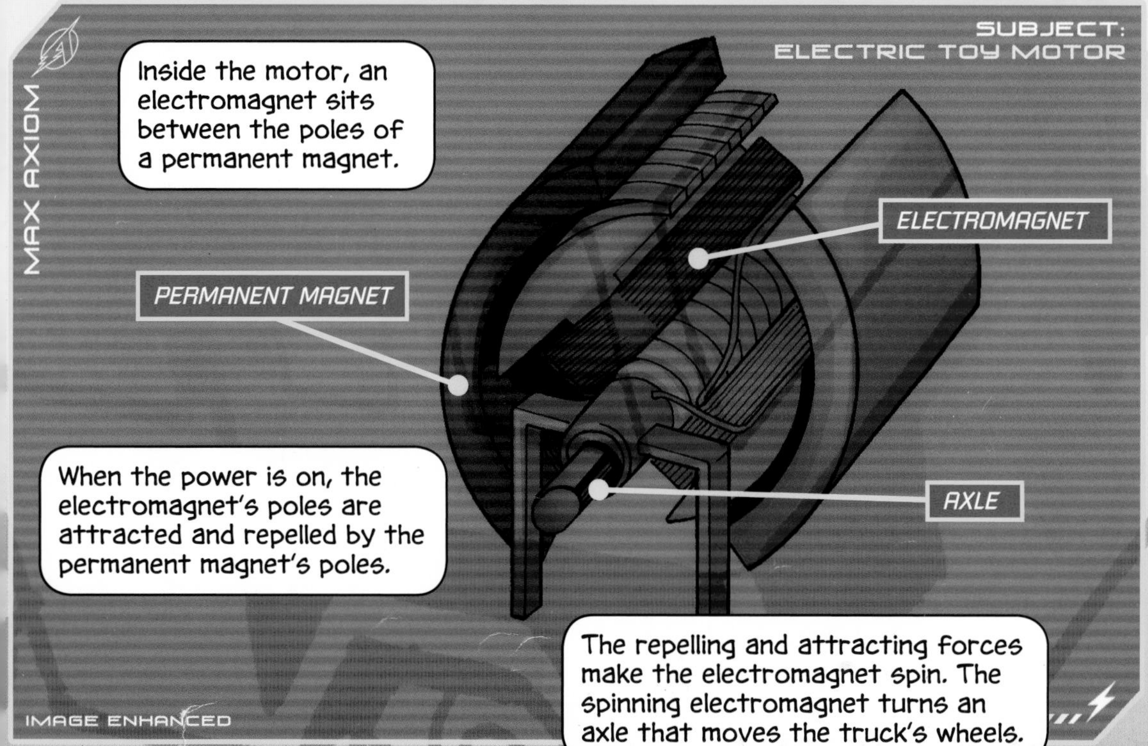
SUBJECT:
ELECTRIC TOY MOTOR
MAX AXIOM
Inside the motor, an electromagnet sits between the poles of a permanent magnet.
ELECTROMAGNET
PERMANENT MAGNET
AXLE
When the power is on, the electromagnet's poles are attracted and repelled by the permanent magnet's poles.
The repelling and attracting forces make the electromagnet spin. The spinning electromagnet turns an axle that moves the truck's wheels.
IMAGE ENHANCED

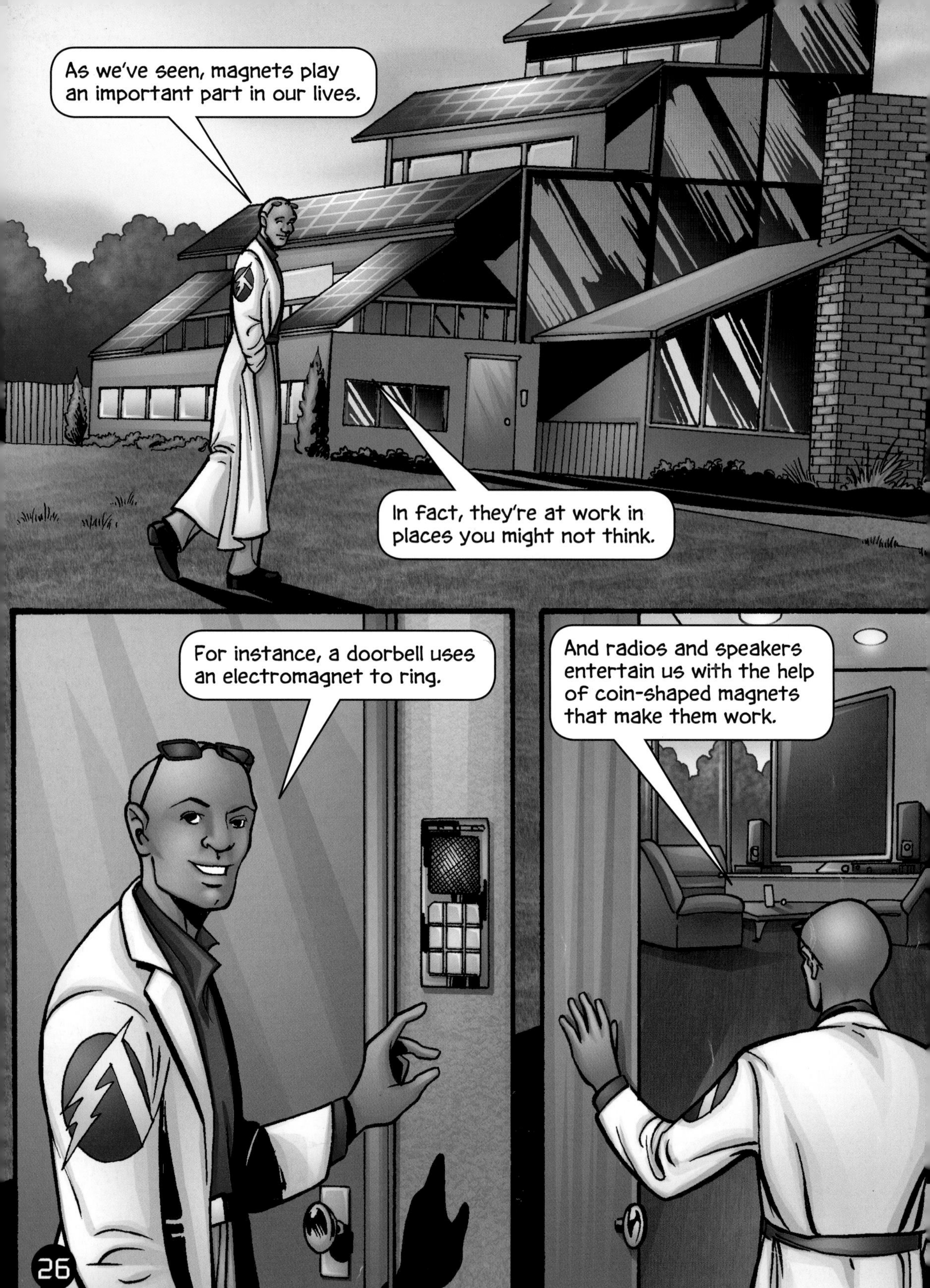
As we've seen, magnets play an important part in our lives.
In fact, they're at work in places you might not think.
For instance, a doorbell uses an electromagnet to ring.
And radios and speakers entertain us with the help of coin-shaped magnets that make them work.

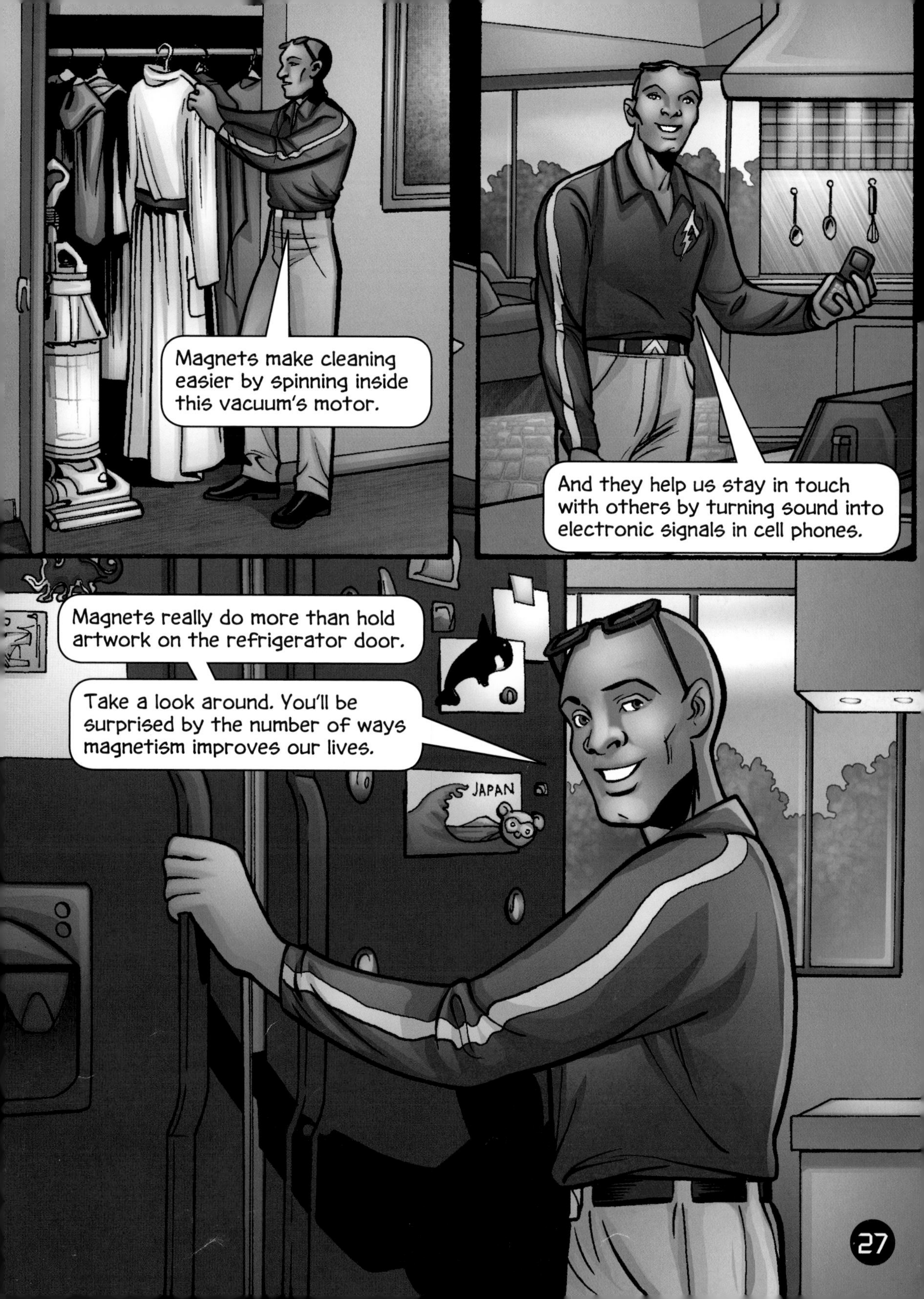
Magnets make cleaning easier by spinning inside this vacuum's motor.
And they help us stay in touch with others by turning sound into electronic signals in cell phones.
Magnets really do more than hold artwork on the refrigerator door.
Take a look around. You'll be surprised by the number of ways magnetism improves our lives.
JAPAN

MORE ABOUT MAGNETISM

Some animals sense earth's magnetic field and use it to help them find their way. Whales, dolphins, and many birds use earth's magnetic field during migration. Australia's compass termites always build their nests facing north.

Earth's north magnetic pole has moved about 700 miles (1,127 kilometers) since it was first discovered in 1831. If it continues moving at its current speed and direction, the north magnetic pole will be located in Siberia by 2050.

Some farmers make their cattle swallow a magnet to keep them healthy. This small magnet attracts nails and pieces of wire they accidentally eat while grazing. The magnet keeps the bits of metal from passing through their stomachs and damaging their other organs.

The National High Magnetic Field Laboratory at Florida State University in Tallahassee has the world's largest magnet. This giant magnet stands 16 feet (5 meters) tall and weighs more than 30,000 pounds (13,608 kilograms). Scientist developed the magnet for 13 years at a cost of $16.5 million.

The sun has a very strong magnetic field. Over time, this field gets knotted and twisted creating dark-colored sunspots on the sun's surface. Sunspots always come in pairs. One is a north magnetic pole while the other is a south magnetic pole.

The sun's magnetic field flips every 11 years. The north magnetic pole becomes a south magnetic pole and the south magnetic pole becomes a north magnetic pole.

 Can a magnet attract a penny? Not a United States penny. U.S. pennies are made mostly of zinc and copper. Neither zinc nor copper is magnetic. British pennies are another story. They are made mostly of steel coated with a thin layer of copper. A magnet will easily pick up British pennies because magnets attract steel.

MORE ABOUT

SUPER SCIENTIST

Real name: Maxwell J. Axiom
Hometown: Seattle, Washington
Height: 6' 1"   Weight: 192 lbs
Eyes: Brown   Hair: None

Super capabilities: Super intelligence; able to shrink to the size of an atom; sunglasses give x-ray vision; lab coat allows for travel through time and space.

Origin: Since birth, Max Axiom seemed destined for greatness. His mother, a marine biologist, taught her son about the mysteries of the sea. His father, a nuclear physicist and volunteer park ranger, schooled Max on the wonders of earth and sky.

One day on a wilderness hike, a megacharged lightning bolt struck Max with blinding fury. When he awoke, Max discovered a newfound energy and set out to learn as much about science as possible. He traveled the globe earning degrees in every aspect of the field. Upon his return, he was ready to share his knowledge and new identity with the world. He had become Max Axiom, Super Scientist.

Glossary

atom (AT-uhm)—an element in its smallest form

domain (doh-MAYN)—a group of magnetic atoms

electromagnet (e-lek-troh-MAG-nit)—a temporary magnet created when an electric current flows through a conductor

electron (e-LEK-tron)—a tiny particle in an atom that travels around the nucleus

magma (MAG-muh)—melted rock found beneath the surface of earth

magnetic field (mag-NET-ik FEELD)—the area around a magnet that has the power to attract magnetic metals

magnetite (MAG-nuh-tite)—a hard, black rock found in earth that attracts iron; magnetite is also known as lodestone.

magnetosphere (mag-NET-ohs-sfir)—the magnetic field extending into space around a planet or star

nucleus (NOO-klee-uhss)—the center of an atom; a nucleus is made up of neutrons and protons.

pivot (PIV-uht)—a point on which something turns or balances

pole (POHL)—one of the two ends of a magnet; a pole can also be the top or bottom part of a planet.

repel (ri-PEL)—to push apart; like poles of magnets repel each other.

temporary (TEM-puh-rer-ee)—lasting only a short time

READ MORE

Cooper, Christopher. *Magnetism: From Pole to Pole.* Science Answers. Chicago: Heinemann Library, 2004.

Morgan, Ben. *Magnetism.* Elementary Physics. San Diego: Blackbirch Press, 2003.

Nelson, Robin. *Magnets.* First Step Nonfiction. Minneapolis: Lerner, 2004.

Parker, Steve. *Opposites Attract: Magnetism.* Everyday Science. Chicago. Heinemann Library, 2005.

Richardson, Adele. *Magnetism: A Question and Answer Book.* Questions and Answers: Physical Science. Mankato, Minn.: Capstone Press, 2006.

INTERNET SITES

FactHound offers a safe, fun way to find Internet sites related to this book. All of the sites on FactHound have been researched by our staff.

Here's how:
1. Visit *www.facthound.com*
2. Choose your grade level.
3. Type in this book ID **1429601418** for age-appropriate sites. You may also browse subjects by clicking on letters, or by clicking on pictures and words.
4. Click on the **Fetch It** button.

FactHound will fetch the best sites for you!

INDEX